The Garden Hut

by Carmel Reilly
illustrated by Leo Trinidad

OXFORD
UNIVERSITY PRESS

Costa and Vanda went into the backyard.

“We need a little garden hut,” said Vanda.

"It can go next to the fish pond,"
said Costa. "The sand is soft."

Costa and Vanda went to the shed.

"Look, big bits of card!" said Vanda.

Vanda and Costa shifted the card.

Just then, Vanda lost her grip.

The card sank into the pond.

“I think this is too damp,” said Costa.

"There is some carpet in the shed," said Vanda. "That might do."

They went back to the shed.

"Can we lift it up?" said Costa.

"Yes," said Vanda. "We can."

Vanda and Costa hung up the carpet.

Champ the cat went to look.

“No, Champ, stop!” said Vanda.

The carpet fell down.

Vanda went back to the shed.
"A pillow hut?" she said.

The pillows were too soft.

"What can we do now?" Vanda said.

"We can put up the tent," said Costa.

"What tent?" said Vanda.

"There," said Costa. "On the bench!"

“Help me put it up!” said Vanda.

“Sure!” said Costa.

"A garden hut!" said Costa. "With carpet and pillows."

"And a bed for Champ," said Vanda.

Look Back

Encourage students to use the pictures to retell the story.